Poetically Inking

Just Me, My Pen & the Mic

Kim B Miller

All of these copyrighted poems were created by Kim B Miller and they cannot be reproduced, copied, used, transmitted, or sold in any way, shape or form without the written consent of the author. All rights are reserved.

© Copyright 2015 Kim B. Miller.
All Rights Reserved.

Dedication

I'd like to dedicate this book to all of the people who have touched my soul and to God for allowing me to experience life and express it in words.

Table of Contents

Name	Page
1. My World	1
2. Getting Married	5
3. Almost	9
4. My Song	13
5. Bye	17
6. The New "Man"	21
7. Lost Sistahs	25
8. Treyvon	29
9. Mother-Daughter	35
10. Gone	39
11. Side Piece	43
12. Hurt	47
13. Husband & Wife	51
14. American Blackness	55
15. My Pen	59
16. Get Gone	63
17. Brown Jail	67
18. Dear Black People	71
19. Limited Vision	77
20. The Mirror	81
21. Dear Ladies	85
22. Dear Fellas	91
23. His-story	97
24. Found but Lost	101
25. You Don't Get Me	105
26. Transformers	109
27. Dear Dad	115
28. I'm Black	119
29. Our Kids	123
30. The Beatitudes	127
Haiku	131
Kimism	137

MY

WORLD

Take a gaze through my eyes

Envision our world reinvented

Walk with me through my Eden

Slowly examine the simplistic beauty that surrounds us

Take a moment and walk with me… in this world…

Men have returned to "Adamistic" interpretations

Spiritual cohesion and thoughts encased

Vision simplistically clear, all gray dissipated

Their temple is fortified steel not easily penetrated

Cemented distortions once chipped, now broken have crumbled under truth

For in this world…

A man's worth is not based on a number that follows a dollar sign

A man's stature is not based on a title that fits on a plaque

A man's love is not based on momentary physical exchanges

What he drives will not get him to his true destination Heaven so it is irrelevant

The respect elasticity previously used on men has been rescinded

Their roots do not plant seed vicariously in fertile soil

Leaves don't fall when a perfumed scent descends upon them
The tree just as it stands is unwavering
For the tree does not bend to get fruit
Here men look for a complete, multidimensional partners
Instead of a characteristic show pieces
Undefinable titles that enslaved men are not recited here
So money is not linked with importance
In your world death is the only time that the realization of life is observed
In my Eden we live in life the way you write in death
Wrapped in the knowledge the sisterhood has gained,
Eve's descendants stand ever vigilant
No longer accessories to male vision
Standing in pride, wrapped in esteem, covered in glory
Unwrapping us is a gift not an assumption
When a fully rooted, spiritual compasses stands we are realized
In this world women are not entities
A woman's worth is not based her temple
Women are not materialistic mannequins
No disrespect is offered and none is accepted
Self-worth is embedded, not lyrically persuaded

Knowledge and capability are the standards for our growth

We are not the sum of your desires

We are not background material to your life's script

We are substance

All distinctions have evolved here

Everyone owns fault, no hypocrisy

Right and wrong supersede status

Forgiveness overtakes hate

Yes, it's all here, it's all possible in this domain

Light rules here and darkness is relegated to the back

This world is obtainable but this is not a one person revolution

We all are the catalyst

The only restraint to realization is complacency

Fear will not overwhelm our spiritual strength

It needs willing prey

My vision does not allow for its existence but fear rules this world

The work, the determination, the structure to achieve this transformation is not manufactured, it is right here

We can breathe this stagnant air or surpass our own limits

The vision is real

The new reality already exist we just don't live in it

GETTING

MARRIED

The love that you seek is not here

I can't offer inner peace to you it is not mine to give

I am not your Savior your prayers don't come to me

I am not your everything for that would make you nothing

I cannot create a receptacle of hope and implant it in you

I can cultivate it but I can't initiate it

Perfuming my ears with lustful words is not love

Joy does not start and end on my lips

Happiness is not a fix delivered in doses

I cannot be your drug dealer

No one can sustain that, love starts within but you can't dip into that hollow shell and scrap love out

You have been listening to wrong so long when right is quoted you don't even recognize it

This union is supposed to be between two that become one

Love can't be drained, it needs to flow

Don't blame me for your lack of love

That vessel was empty before I picked it up

You thought a ring would solve this

Jewelry does not penetrate the soul

The echo you hear reverberating is from your emptiness

Your inner prison has convicted you

Love was no taken from you

You never had it

Love only needs one companion to exist, you but you want me to resuscitate it

Breathing love back into your flesh, absorbing, it like air

Love me without extending your legs

You are not the sum of your parts

I know your life's picture was not painted with perfect strokes

Yet you are what I want, my eternity rest with you but not like this

I am not so consumed by you that I don't grasp you

This transfusion ends today

You are standing right in front of me yet I miss you

You cannot find every answer from your heart in my soul

Why do you insist in being a painting of a picture of the drawing of a reflection of you

I'm looking for the king of my throne not the back of my heal

Look through your heartache and see what stands before you

True love with her hand open waiting for you to grab it

ALMOST

I almost paused and looked at the bright sun shining down from above

I hear the sky was so bright it looked like a large painting with beautiful white inflections but I just ignored God's radiance

I almost went to view my child embrace and overcome her fears

She glows from the realization that she is capable but work consumed my time

I almost parted my lips to expound on the sheer joy you bring to my heart Lord but I didn't want to be judged a fanatic

So I just smiled and said a silent prayer

I almost went to see those who sculptured the clay that is me but I lingered in empty excuses

Now regrets are what I face

I almost took time to explore the calling that permeates my inner soul

Instead I watched other people live their dream

Precious years evaporated away

I almost taught my fruit, life lessons and Biblical truths

Instead I let them cultivate their own meaning

Now they don't know the Living Word

I almost took time to look past my fears to my God given talents but I let doubt infuse my mind

I am lost and I have no sense of direction

I almost took time to notice imperfections in my heart and words

Defiance was my response

I pulled away and isolated myself

I almost took time to strengthen my earthly temple but I was too busy

So I am barely standing here before you today

I know you're thinking I almost died but you are wrong

I almost lived

MY

SONG

There is a song that only I know

You can't hear it

My song is wrapped in baggage

It is not a lullaby, it is hateful and cruel

I wrote the lyrics

No one else could write them because you don't know me

I'm not what you see

Don't let the reflection that I allow to seep out persuade you

This is a painting of me not an echo of my inner being

I'm not strong and brave, I am underwater gasping for air

Don't you realize I've always lived there

You have never seen me beside you because I am beneath you

I am not you

Stop pushing me to be phenomenal, everyone can't be amazing

Some of us are not destined for greatness

My acceptance of that sustains me

You want to feed me hope

I've already regurgitated love so hope can't exist here

I won't let it

This is my song, my internal dialogue

I wrote down every note, I know the words

I am useless, I am nothing

I shouldn't even be inhabiting the same space as you

I wrote it down just like you said it to me, Momma

I didn't forget a single note

Don't worry, you don't have to sing it anymore

I got it now

I will not let you down, I will be exactly what you said

I have embodied your words

I'm so insignificant I am indistinguishable from the background

I am fading away, fading away

Has my melody left you silent

Don't burden yourself absorbed in me

Focus on the ones entangled with your lyrics

All of you wrote songs for your children

They are rehearsing it now

What lyrics did you donate

Your legacy is your words, you are the author

They just can't see you, they only see what they are not

That is their song

Can you stop singing it, can you stop singing it, can you stop singing it

BYE

Slowly I turn struggling to breath

Trying to stay relevant

Time has been generous but I have not

I have drifted toward isolation

Hope is a distant companion

It took love with it

I used to trust so fluently

It was freely given but the flow back seemed strained

So I focused on my temple

A name befitting its worship

I ignored anything that did not increase my admiration

Fixated on the shell I contaminated my yolk

Devoting time to the body and none to the soul caused artificial contentment

There was measured deception aimed at my heart

That was the whisper replayed in my head

Darkness shut out any radiance

Hope returned to sacrifice her dignity

Determined to bring back the light in my eyes

I would not allow the air from her lips to hit my ears

Now I am slowly fading away

I have no one

I'm with no one

My last vision of life will be this unadorned ceiling

Slowly I press my eyes close

I question every moment

Faith assumed over time has disappeared

Tears fall and regrets build though I resist both

I can't make it out

Loud bursts of light

Subtlety, softness

Slowly drifting I feel emptiness

I don't want to die alone

Even my arrogance has left me

I can't breath

I can't see

The darkness is consuming me

I wish I had…

Live today or die today with wishes pressed into your lips

THE

NEW "MAN"

Grasping the bricks used to construct our future

Our foundation incomplete

Altering the paths we walk by hindering our steps

Our journey unfinished but our awareness intensified

The "man's" agenda exposed

Limit the pigmentation

Individual casualties encompass too much time

Psychological warfare started

Infinite uses, massive devastation

Obstruct one man and he may overcome

Hinder all men and limit the race

The domino tipped is still dropping intended targets

Slowly pushing more off their purpose

The "man" takes recognition

Nameless, faceless but known to all

Proud fighters assimilated

Kunta unrecognizable to our ears

We are lost, lost where we are found

Circulating our own drain

We're so busy eating ass soup

We don't realize all of the water ain't dirty

Hope flickers, the flame getting dynamic

Dominoes waiting to be knocked down step out

The chain is fragmented

No longer eating the agenda being fed

Buffalo no longer running on command but not leaving either, stagnantly looking for purpose

Fixated on material things while others move toward world domination

Quoting we're ready for the revolution but the only thing we do is revolve around ourselves

Looking at clothing as a Savior

Wearing importance instead of earning it

Finishing verses as long as they are not in the Bible

Quoting Biggie and Tupac like they are scholars

Trading one slavery for another

Once Kings and Queens now the kingdom is open

Yet we focus on the robe and chariots while others look toward the throne

History revisited

No focus on knowledge

No knowledge gained

No learning done

Assimilation complete

The "man" that held us back is dead

We are the new man

LOST

SISTAHS

Money is the root to all evil

Don't let it be the only roots you recognize

A legacy of fortitude seeds our past

Our roots secured to strong Sistahs who came before us

Bethune, Tubman, Chisolm, Walker, Coleman

Some of whose name you won't recognize

Since their ass ain't being slapped in a music video

Their importance erased like the invisible black ink they were written in

Forced to be called names, we now embrace

Fighting for dignity, that we no longer command

Their backs broken, bent over so we could stand strong

The slavery mentality in our head got us craving a master

This master money

Doing anything to make more paper

The bottom line in our bank statement our only focus

Riding any pole to increase it

Trying to use sex to be successful

Though spelled the same the **penis** is not the only ladder to success the **pen is**

Trying to twerk our way to importance

You can't light a spark under your ass rubbing your thighs together

Soul Suicide almost complete

So lyrically intertwined that we believe the words we hear

I'm under water but I'm breathing fine

Stop, listening to a legend does not make you one

Your lungs are fighting to expand

Your ear drums slowly losing their rhythm

Living lyrical fantasies has you drowning

The curve in your back is not a road map to victory

Stand up and look at the commanding flowers that once blossomed

There are no weeds on this fertile ground

One seat not vacated made the whole world stand and take notice

One conductor without a train made freedom free

Judged not for shape or size

They did not die to sanction ass-ittude

Rosa didn't expose her breast so she could sit

Harriet didn't have a man cosign her train… **They stood**

Red, black and green aren't needed for pride

Black stands good all by itself

Lost Sistahs your roots are calling

Can you stop dropping like it hot

Bringing boys to the yard

Stop licking the lollipop

Long enough to get your self-respect back

African queens pick up your crowns

Black does not have to be bent over to be seen

Ignorance embraced

You know to put your hand up with a ring on it but know nothing about putting your fist up with some pride on it

Pray a man your way

You can't sex someone into loving you

Love your reflection and deny the hatred

Your skin is not too dark, your hair is not too short, your hips are not too wide

You are a Spirit filled African American queen

Send back the scraps and realize your worth

If you don't want no scrubs

Stop bending down to pick one up

Come home lost Sistahs

Our circle is incomplete

Until all Sistahs find their way home

One lost sheep is one too many

TREYVON

Last night I had a dream that I spoke to Trayvon Martin

He looked so real, I tried not to stare

I asked him if he was hurt and he said not yet

Water escaped my eyes streaming down my cheeks

He grabbed my hand and said no time to cry

Remember death only hurts the living

Hatred only grows where it is welcome

Terror needs a host to act

Terror without a terrorist is just a word but impurities can evolve, pain can ignite justice

Justice with a driven purpose

I know my fate

My purpose was forced upon me by a man I didn't know

With a prejudice I did not see

And a gun he ought not have

For a law that should not stand

I did not plan on being the product of unjustified fear

But I ended up with an unwanted companion, hate

Hate followed me, cornered me and fought me

Truth tried to intervene

I battled to breathe, to make it home

I fought but you already know hate will win

When I take my last breath hate is going to smile feeling victorious but that will not be my last vision

I see possibilities, I see hope and love flashing before me like burst of bright light

Hate will not be happy it wants to seep in and consume my soul, controlling my destiny

I will tell him you may take the air I breathe but not the light I shine

He will be speechless at my resolve

Hate will get his canvass out and paint a picture of me

I was a thug, a monster

Monsters scare people because they have unlimited fear

Hate will draw a picture of himself and try to pass it off as me

My parents thought they would be standing alone but love showed up in massive quantities

My non existing presence will be recognized

My truth told

My picture will be repainted

Not with perfect strokes but with truth

I was prey

I was hunted

I was assassinated by hate

One hoodie away from greatness

My future is gone but my spiritual legacy is undetermined

Fear blurred the lines

Loudly spinning cotton like it was certainty

Designing fiction to surpass truth

Lies erased, rewritten, erased, unreadable

Discarding truth, like skin, removable but still relevant

My eyes have seen past death

I envision restored devotion

Not in an unjust justice system

Not in earthly punishment

Not in standing ground over someone else

This was never a black and white storm

This is about red, white and blue, freedom, plain and simple

Blaming an entire race puts you under the same umbrella hate was carrying

Don't hate in my name

Don't use me to push your agenda

I've been used enough

Hate fears retribution

Hate fears truth

Hate fears hate

My time is short

Live your life embracing every second

Remember hate can be anywhere but so can love

I have to go

Wait Trayvon ………. (gunshot)

One hoodie away from greatness

MOTHER

DAUGHTHER

Mother

Do you even recognize the flow of hate

When was the last time you said thank you and but did not soon follow

Hypocrisy surging through your veins

Fully oxygenated viciousness spread daily

Respectful to none but the mirror

Spiting lyrical toughness but useless to your own evolution

Be thankful or be quiet

Daughter

Well, I hear your lyrics but that's not my song

I am fruit picked directly from the tree that now denounces my existence

You took me with you everywhere, except church

Kanye walking with Jesus taught me more than you

Duplicity is a family recipe and I learned from the best

A foundation built on ass will not stand

In dick you trust

Yet you look at me with discerning eyes

Close your thighs and maybe we can talk

I can't even recognize you standing up since I've always seen you on your back

If hypocrisy is this family's tree, clearly I am not the only leaf clinging to its roots

The only thing you taught me was to keep my legs tone and my ass tight

The only class you taught was the art of men and my body is the center of the universe

I have King Kong on a bracelet

His balls are my earrings

Inspiration to greatness, a reminder of possibilities

So you said

I'm no anomaly, I am my mother's daughter

I looked toward you, I lived what I learned and I saw

I'm a home grown hooker

Now step off pimp before I forget you brought me into this world

You painted this Da-Vinci

Now step back and enjoy your artwork

GONE

Can you just stop for a minute

Why aren't I enough for you

I did everything you asked

I changed to suit you

I lost friends and weight

My hair dyed and my dignity

I talked low not to overshadow you

All I need is a smile from your face and the once still world starts to revolve

Your love covers me

So completely that I don't even know who else is present when you are with me

I gasp for air when you are not facing me

I need you

I became the circumference of your desires

So how can you walk away so painlessly

Please tell me

Well, I never wanted you to change

I just wanted you

You turned into a desire created in your heart not mine

All I wanted was you and all you wanted was you

There was never any room for me in your heart

You already live there

You don't want me

You want the love you created in your head

A dialogue known only to you

I'm just a drawing you etched to appease your ego

I am the accessory you put on and rip off

I really didn't think you would even notice I was gone

I'm a prop in your life's play

What performance am I missing

It doesn't matter

I won't be here for the next curtain call

I was never really here

You don't know anything about me

Tell me something

What is my sacred space

What is my passion, my experiences, my inner fears

Just as I thought

You don't even realize I'm not even here

I left a week ago

Your emotions are so contaminated you have envisioned me, still here

I'm not here this is your blurred reality

You have to stop saying stay

I'm already gone

SIDE

PIECE

You think my clay was made for you to mold

My body yours to command

I told myself you were the one to heal my wounded soul

You want to heal with just a kiss

And strengthen with just a glance

I don't want to expose my eyes to the light

The dream is more beautiful but I can't live with my eyes sealed

Truth bleeding out with every blink

Completely envying lies

Mountain climbing for the wrong cause

Sipping lust through a straw

Words so strong he got me lyrically licking my lips

Spiritual awareness looking for affection

One step away from an epiphany

Love slaughtered so I can bask in lust

Keeping me suppressed

He can pump it (hips) but he can't pump it (heart)

He can't touch me, without touching me

He is lost without his hands, I am lost without his touch

His existence enabling mine

Awareness coherent in between blinks of ecstasy

Blurred lines leading him back to my flesh

While stagnant air chokes my soul

Questions lingering on my tongue

My heart echoing emptiness

While someone else's man lies in my bed

He's who I want right now

20 years later the right has faded but the now has stayed

Betrayal served nightly

Dignity dripping away with every drop of sweat

Beautifying scraps while the main course is served elsewhere

Dodging truth like bullets

Telling myself I am his world

Unless ass is a hemisphere I am not it

I'm not a mistress

I'm a 20 year afterthought scheduled at his convenience

HURT

I don't know your momma or your daddy

I look at you and I wonder

Who formed you

You are solidified pain covered in beauty

Running from love

Like it's a slave master trying to rip skin off your back

Covering shame embedded in your soul

Cutting hate on the same line you do cocaine

Inhaling both to get your fix

Rejecting love because that's not the four letter word that suits you

Badgering your heart for beating

I look and I see greatness

You look and you see nothing

Yet we are both looking at you

One step away from self-imposed cannibalism

You don't want to stop the bleeding

You want to see the brilliance of its flow

Limiting love's air

Hoping it will take its last breath

Love can't commit suicide

It has to be murdered but you ain't no murder

You're a serial killer

Slaughtering every ounce of love sent your way

You have fought for isolation and won

Home grown agony is all you eat

Loathing the sight of your own reflection

Avoiding the mirror

Does not change the view

Get to the root of your pain

Stop cutting off leaves hoping the roots will die

If that little girl in you cries out again

Let her know the truth

The monster is not under the bed

She sleeps in it

HUSBAND

WIFE

Pre-poem

He's just got home from work and helped his wife fold some letters. She also gave him his favorite drink just the way he likes it. She stopped briefly and said, "I want to read you one of the letters you just helped me fold. It will explain how I've been felling lately".

……………………………………………………..

I've been battling to breathe

I'm just existing moment to moment

Life is a weight pressing down on my chest

I don't want to breathe in air no meant for me

I am walking through life like I've been sentenced to live

My painted on happiness has been muddied by truth

Cracks eventually exposing my façade

Now raw and unprotected I am vulnerable

Listening for my heartbeat I only hear a rhythm I want gone

Silence the screams coming from my soul

I'd give all I have for a second of silence

Pain is all I know and I let it consume me

You could not have saved me

I've been waiting for this cliff for a long time

It's finally my turn to jump

I just wish you could see through my eyes

Your love is something that I could not absorb

Sorrow is all I see

Darkness is closing in and I will succumb to it

My last breath is soon upon me

He paused and looked at me

Don't do this

Your pain is real I can see that now

I noticed your once vibrant aura has weakened

Give me time to rejuvenate your joy

Don't cut life short, let me comfort you through this pain

Oh I think you misunderstood

That's not my suicide note, it's yours

Thanks for folding it for me earlier

I'll make sure I get your letter

Right about now you should feel your muscles starting to tighten

Your breath getting shallow

Your vision getting blurry

Now I'd love to stay and watch as life slowly drains from your poisoned body

But it looks like my best friend, your mistress is feeling suicidal also

AMERICAN

BLACKNESS

Oh say can you see

We see blackness thrown to the ground and dragged through injustice

Truth is a beautiful mistress seldom seen in the skin we are in

We see black and blue only come together to make bruises

Victims scrutinized

Implicated in their own destruction

Truth being choked out

Dig long enough until you find some black dirt to throw

Black blood can't penetrate a blue wall

We have the right to remain silent known more than Lift Every Voice & Sing

Truth Untold

Blur our edges with your racist charcoal

But don't sketch our story with a lie dipped in truth

Stories edited

History altered to diminish our contributions

Hated but emulated

Natural black farm fed asses duplicated

Actual uses extend pass twerking, clapping and visual stimulation

Proudly we hail

Not hail to chief since a black man got in the oval office

Ridiculed like none other

Birth certificate scrutinized more than Nixon's deceptions were publicized

And those broad stripes and…

The stripes we embody in prison instituted blackness

Where it's a felony to wear a hoodie

And a misunderstanding to pump holes into the person wearing it

The red blood stripes shed by our white brother and sisters

Fighting to set freedom free

Their involvement whitewashed

Allies separated trying to thin the herd

We have never walked alone

Trying to feed isolation to the black nation

Land of the free

Free to watch our daughter's worth be reduced to butt clapping

Free to sacrifice our sons to trigger happy cops looking for a reason to squeeze

Free to work twice as hard as our counterparts not to be judged inferior

Too dark to employ but not to pigmented to watch your children

Home of the brave

Bravely watching crap get turned into truth

Fragmented bull crap still stinks

Land stripped away from brave Native American warriors

Blacks ain't the first race America has bent over

Adjust your vision America

Our blackness does not need fixing

We are in a movement but the movement will not be televised

Exploit blackness take 6 billion, 6 million and 62 (click sign) Action!

MY PEN

Flawed but unique from this tongue I will speak

I use my pen as my sword

My drink is the ink that flows from each blink

Liquor can't do nothing that my pen can't

My pen can heighten your senses with words dripping with sensuality

100 proof colors flowing out of its tip

Changing your mood by the way that I sway it

Yes, this pen is armed

Ricocheting words of the walls of your ears, to make things clear

Your journey begins at the tip of this pen

This beautiful paper, the ledge I stay in

Staying confined to the lines in my mind I write my truth

My pen forced inside

Guiding each stroke

My mind contracted with each word that I wrote

Coming to an end or yet starting again

Completed, erased, your arousal replaced

Like the Staple Singers, I'll take you there

This pen is relieving what this brain is conceiving

Bleeding ink, my pen sings to me in all bass, no treble

A journey released from my lips to your ears

I hear the drip of ink's tears against my soul's widow

It's my sight without vision

Complete thanks to this pen

This ink does more than you think

GET

GONE

Now you don't like me

I used to be all you thought about

I'm not your cup of tea

I used to be all you wanted to drink

I'm done trying to get you to love me

If I'm not your cup of tea pick another flavor

Are you trying to throw shade on this Sistah

You ain't blocking no light

You need a back with a bone in it to do that

Look you don't qualify for any of this

A Queen and a jackass can't make a prince

I mistook you for a King but now I see you can't even qualify to be a pawn

You thought I was your jump off

You have to be in, in order to jump off

Your temporary, past tense, insignificant ass was never in

My legs are just like your mind, closed to small content

You were supposed to ignite passion in my soul

You said you were my soul mate but you don't care about my soul

You only care about mating

The street light is on so it's time for you to go

The well – "come" mat was not meant for you

Hit delete, you've been erased

This Sistah is many things but in love with a temporary scratcher to a long term itch is not one of them

There is no us

I won't be that woman

You know the one who mourns the relationship she thought she had that never existed

The one who prays for greatness but settles for you

I don't have to break the chain

I just need to let go of the weakest link

My name ain't Plato, I don't sculpt men

Men have to be complete when they show up

I want you to savor the flavor of my words lingering on your lips

Hear me with a crispness that removes all doubt

I looked over my existence with you and saw emptiness

There is no song in my heart that plays your lyrics

But I think this one suits this situation right here

I think you better call, text, or skype Tyrone

But you can't use my phone

BROWN

JAIL

Don't leave me here

Take me with you

I need you

We'll get through this

I have to go

I'll be back

I don't know how to explain raw pain

The pain of leaving a piece of your heart behind a closed door

Watching steel bars separate you from love

First I only saw my son's pain then I looked at this brown prison with no vacancies

Filled with anguish, despair & degust

One brown brother next to another

Like a rope injustice is wrapped around their necks

They sit and wait but the rope tightens

My nourishment irrelevant, time insignificant, breathing labored

My son's unforgettable aura surrounds me

I inhale memories of his childhood

I pray for a victory that will reunite us

Fighting to be heard

Ignored, punished, ridiculed by injustice

Grasping for any hope, I lean on truth

We begin the long journey to restoration

Tried and convicted before one word is said

Skin tone sentenced to life

Guilty till proven guiltier

Innocence never considered

If we had enough money we may be relevant but still guilty

I press forward

My cry turns into a scream

No walls, glass or paper can separate us

I will fight for you until fighting to breathe is all I have left

Our hearts cannot be separated by words written on a judge's paper

No ink can write I love you large enough to match what I feel for my children

My love for you is the one thing that has no flaws

Hear me son

You are beautiful

I miss you

I fought for you

You were worth it

You are worth it

You're my son

DEAR BLACK

PEOPLE

Dear Black People

History was once our constant companion but now she sits in isolation with very few visitors

We need to reconnect to our roots and restore history to her rightful place in our hearts and minds

Let me be clear

History is not only available in February, during TV commercials, in 30 second intervals

Beware, the new master is ignorance

We put him in charge and we keep him in place

We pledge allegiance to rappers and singers and wonder why ignorance flows

We overlook the connections in place

History and freedom are sisters with two different fathers

Some have sculpted the past to fit their future

A limited vision looking back causes limited vision looking forward but whose vision is getting blurred

Blacks and whites picketed, marched, and died together

There wasn't just black blood spilled but some would like us to erase history that way we feel isolated and alone

Truth be told, others want to bury their hatred in white soil

Trying to hang the sins of the father on their sons

Sounds like a new black master talking to recruit a new set of slaves
We need to start demanding more of ourselves
One demand is to stop making lyrical links to truths in songs
We let the beat sway us even though we know the lyrics will lead to moral decay
Now some rappers and singers have come up with some songs about the revolution
One revolutionary anthem can't undo 50 songs where women are portrayed as nothing more than blow up pornographic Barbie dolls, only useful for sexual pleasure
What will we be next week, will we be back to our hoe status or will we still be righteous Sistahs
Where are the proceeds from these songs going
Is it going to secure freedom for anyone who is oppressed or is it just another beat to distract us from the fact that many of them aren't getting involved
We don't need another song about the revolution
We need more soldiers on the field
They don't want to get their hands dirty or their Gucci shoes soiled with marching dirt
Yet some complain Sharpton hasn't done enough
Stop looking for someone else to have your revolution

We are on the sidelines waiting to reap the benefits of a war we didn't participate it
Yet we have time to critique the workers in the field
If you don't like what they are doing put your "mouse" down and pick your ass up
A movement does not end with one person but it can start with one
If you want a movement hit them in the pocket
Green walks across all lines
I feel I need to have a class today because so many people are eating the bull they are being fed
Some are rehashing it and serving it to others, as truth
If black lives mattered you would not need a hashtag and a cardboard sign to make it true
America, black people do not go around looking for hate
We point out the hate that you ignore
There are no qualifications to see hate and not like it
You see the news refuse to state our views, especially when we're one of the accused
You can't put an entire race under one umbrella
If you have a problem direct your anger at the one who caused it not the race who wears it

This is not my country white of thee sweet land of "black-idy" of thee I sing, stop it

America, we don't let the media dictate who our enemies are

So you'd have to drag us kicking and screaming to "Stupidity Ave" yet some many people live on that street voluntarily

America the truth is in the light

The facts are in the light

So if you're in the dark it's because you turned out the lights (click)

Even my vision of my people has changed

When I see black faces

I see dead people

Dead from ignorance

Dead from hatred

Dead from police officer's bullets

Dying, Dying, Dying, Dead

What are you waiting for officer

Take your chalk and write on this blackboard and erase her existence

We already know Shonda was not the first one to write

How to get away with murder

LIMITED VISION

We gaze at life with limited vision

Staring away from the blind spots in our view

We form opinions based on little thought

Imposing our view on unsuspecting strangers

They don't even realize our preconceived judgments have put them in a box

One they cannot escape

We put our shades on

Vision obstructed because truth is inconvenient

Trying to claim ignorance as a friend

Until injustice spits in our face and we can no longer look away

We walk in the light for the first time, this is what we see

We thought cars were safe

Greed supersedes safety

Recalls delayed but bonuses for executives, paid on time

No recall on death though

Why is a war more profitable than peace

If politicians children had to fight in the front line of every war would we still go

Or is the dollar more important than blood lines

If senators think minimum wage is too high

Why do all of them earn more than that

Let's lower their salaries to what they think we should make

Looking down can sometimes skew your view

Let's examine why they get to vote themselves increases while voting us decreases

Some imply that Obama is one of the worst presidents

Really, are we judging facts or pigmentation

Even if you think he put the country in a ditch

Where was it when Bush left the Grand Canyon

Why aren't truth and justice best friends

Convicting the wrong person leaves the real perpetrator free

Arrest numbers and conviction rates are more important than truth

Truth is an inconvenience that is manipulated and tortured until it is unrecognizable

If Walmart prices are so low and profits are so high
Why are their employees so broke
Pay them a decent wage
Cut one of the executive bonuses, company retreats and up their salaries
People who work should not be just as poor as people who don't

You can't put those rose colored glassed back on now
You've seen too much
They used to smell like roses but now they smell like deception
We are a broken society that needs fixing
We say we want peace and justice
Are we willing to do anything uncomfortable to get it
How can you ask for peace or justice globally when you don't even speak to your sister, brother, cousin, neighbor because they are Black, White, Irish, gay, Jewish…
Insert your own prejudice
You can ignore me but I suggest you escape the confines of your ass and look around before the next cause, news story or hashtag is you

THE

MIRROR

The best way to destroy beauty is from within

That's why the serpent seeks entry into your soul

You've been told to guard your body but your legs don't open themselves

The mind does

You allow his words to seduce you

You only want to go deeper when a man is on top of you but you are silent when he is beside you

Guard you

Some of you guard your phone more than you do your own soul

Drinking words poured into a glass that were made for you

Ugly, fat, useless, unwanted

You keep sipping on them until the flavor becomes natural

You can't even taste disgust

Did you really think that smile hides the cuts on your arms

That scarf covers the marks on your neck

That fake assurance covers the black eye on your soul

Wipe the residue of manure off your lips

Licking someone else's ass has consequences

If you're so right, so flawless

Why don't you believe it

Sing Beyonce's song your way, I woke up like this: fake

Looking for excuses for your success instead of reasons

Quoting, I was lucky

You were not lucky

Luck didn't study for weeks, save money, develop strategies, set up her business, and step out of her comfort zone

You are so blind to you

Applauses are muffled by your own self hate

You can't even see right and you in the same sentence

You blame everyone else but they never forced their ass into your mouth

You volunteered to be Charmin

You are where you put yourself

Others may have started the melody that you are living by but you added the words

If self-hate was a major you'd have a PHD

Stop looking at everyone else as the reason for your pain

You can only get stepped on if you are laying down

You thought guarding your soul against them would keep you safe

Who guards your soul from you

DEAR LADIES

Dear Ladies

I understand some of you are frustrated because your search of a good man has left you empty

But is there a problem with the candidates or the interviewer

I listened to your despair of past loves as you floated on a lake of disgust

Your heart repairing itself yet again

Then I stepped away to see through masculine vision

The portrait painted seldom matches the model

We are the keepers of truth and the destroyer of facts

Our vision distorted, our tongue sharp, our legs open

Let's let truth breath

You say you want strength wrapped in truth's skin

You say you want dependability looking back at you with respect

But who do you extend your hand to

While you quote what you don't want

You look past the very definition of a man and invite boys in his place

Blaming the overlooked man you ignored but not yourself

Lyrically you are well-rehearsed to songs that demand standards

No romance without finance
Requirements based on security wrapped in a bank statement
Instead of love covered with wisdom
Really the lyrics should be you're going to have a j-o-b if you get stuck with me, the high maintenance model
Beauty painted on, padded on and spanked in
Disguised features, hidden flaws
Many of you sang about not wanting "scrubs"
So many woman sang this song proudly, I question why
The sin that eliminates your potential mate is his seat assignment
No carpooling for your man
Disqualifies him from the potential of your great discernment
Ladies didn't many of you get to your destination on the passenger side of your friend's ride
We are known to fly as a collective
So is that hypocritical juice you are sipping on
What if men don't want no "shrub"
A "shrub" is a girl that can't get no love from me
"Butt-clapping" out the passenger side of her best friend's ride trying to holler at me

Flipping the mirror over at us women brings a different perspective

There is a simple way to think about this

If you put honey out, you get bees

If you put sugar down you get ants

If you put ass out you get assholes

You know what I mean

Some woman look for the head before they look at the head

Ladies your foresight was blocked by his foreskin

Remember you said you want a good man or do you just want a man that's good

Here is a good man but you want a playa

That's what you picked

He had a girl when you met him but you took his number anyway

You said his masculinity was enticing you

When he cheated on you your outrage filled the air

He didn't slither his way in

You picked him up

You thought you had a magic vagina that could turn a snake into a man

Now your excuse is you weren't his type

You said he was looking for Beyonce but he really looked
"beyond what you say" and saw what you were willing to
do
I've seen you out there fishing ladies
You disregard honesty for the snake
His tongue sliding across his lips has you intrigued
He showed you who he was
You ignored the genuine for your vision of what he could
be
No man is looking to turn pound cake into soul food
Jump offs don't get a ring they get 3AM booty calls
Some of you already have a good man but you are looking
Don't keep overlooking what you got
A man in hand is worth two in someone else's bush
Good men are sick of being mannequins
Standing in one place waiting to be recognized
Their Godliness ignored
Then here you come broken hearted and hurt because the
ruff neck you picked: hit it and quit it
Now you want the good man to pay for the mistakes you
made when you chose a blatant imitator
We call the imposters dogs
Seldom does a dog go in search of a person

Meaning dogs look for other dogs

Perhaps the fleas you have were already in place

You're the one taking penicillin lattes

The open leg hotel always has room for one more guest

Maybe you can't find a king because he's looking for a queen and not a jump off

He's looking for someone to be his peace not his piece

You got in the word wrong

Look men are painting with imperfect strokes, just like us

Sometimes our limited vision of love is the very reason we don't have it

Love's broad shoulders may be standing right in front of you

Since he doesn't meet your excessive list of "must haves"

You walk around him toward pain

So remember, this the next time you pick a boy instead of a man that guy didn't break your heart, you did

The question is not is he the right man

The real question is are you the right woman

DEAR FELLAS

Dear Fellas

I understand that you are searching for a Queen but your candidates are scarce

Maybe it's because you are only looking at applicants instead of qualifying them

If your true desire is greatness you're going to have to look past your penis to find it

There are woman of God available but you dismiss them when their butt don't clap and their panties don't drop

A queen willing to guard her temple is valuable but not in your mind

Sex is your sole focus

Instead of guiding her to our Heavenly Father you try to get her to call you daddy

Stop worrying about how much semen you can create

Focus on how many amens you can generate

Brother if you want to get somewhere speak to our souls

Our thighs aren't open to interpretation

You don't determine a woman's value based on her size

Some of you have more rigid requirements for your lady than the Olympic qualifying team

Yet you haven't been to the gym in years

If you must have list has a six pack on it you best be in shape yourself
Then there are the fellas who want to rule women
There's only one commander and chief and you ain't it
We ain't looking for daddies we are looking for companions
You need to know what you really want
If you are really looking for someone to clean hire a maid
If you are really looking for someone to cook hire a chef
If you are really looking for someone to ride buy you a horse
If all you want is the cookie there are women out there willing to provide just that
Go find you some rental cookie
Don't pretend to be a King in order to date a Queen and then hit the door before the wet spot dries
If you can't stay for breakfast you shouldn't have asked for "dessert"
Look, women hate fakeness, real is what we crave
Don't imitate or conform to impress us
Assimilate is just like it sounds your ass is late
We can deal with an imperfect man but we need to see who that is

Don't hide him hoping we'll fall in love with a façade of you

Imperfections don't make women leave

Hidden truths make us wonder what else you got buried in your back yard

Some of you can't find love because you're really looking for a cliff note version of a women instead of a full length book

You want something you can pick up on occasion but not someone you get to know from beginning to end

We will not go on a shelf and wait to be picked up at your convenience

Address us with respect

Acknowledge our accomplishments

Approach us with dignity

Stop addressing us like we are sexual organ donors giving up body parts for pleasure

Don't call us thick thighs, fat ass, cherry bottom or any other nastiness the slithers off your tongue

Sistah, Miss and Queen will never fail you

Addressing us by what you see can be used on you as well with blunt, honest consequences

How would you like it if we said...

What's up too short, not getting any, Mr. Not My Type

You must have made a wrong turn the playground is in the back

Then your precious egos would be fractured and in need of repair

Besides you ain't as slick as you think you are

We can see you "playa"

You've been drinking your own Kool-Aid so long you think that you invented a new flavor

Seamen mixed with crap is not new

It's baby formula for boys who haven't learned to walk with real women yet

We just want you to respect who is before you but know this a diamond is still a diamond even if you overlook it

Better yet know that we are not teenagers anymore

So if you're not a King who touches our soul

You won't be touching nothing else

If you want a 24-7 woman you better be willing to give more than 15 minutes to get to know her

We won't slow down our pace to suit your flow

So step up or step off

HIS-STORY

History is pigmented

Black history has a label

A title that segregates us yet again

Our history is not black, our contributions are not black

but we are

We are one of the many trees standing in the forest of life

If you only focus on the color of the tree then you miss the beauty of the forest

So many men stood like these trees, steadfast and unmovable

Some are quick to quote Martin and rightfully so but this forest has more than one prominent tree

Don't just look at the trees that society points to

Overlooked trees have so much relevance

Daniel Hale Williams was a physician who performed the first known open heart surgery

Frederick Jones designed and patented portable air-cooling unit for trucks carrying food

Lewis Latimer is one of the essential inventors of all time, he worked with Edison

Matthew Henson was an explorer best known as the co-discoverer of the North Pole

Mark Dean's IT work led to the development of the color computer monitor

The forest has more trees waiting to be acknowledged

We need to know what we've accomplished to continue on the path that they carved out

Don't wait for the world to point out a tree that is inches from your face

Knowledge is not buried with our ancestors

Learn the facts

Tell another brother or sister so they can prosper

You are trees from the same forest

Each one should teach one

Make the ground stable so your brother is able to accomplish goals through the seed that is planted in him

Some may stumble but trees don't move when another tree falls

They hold each other up

Once we realize that King wasn't the only king we can encourage the young princes

Don't just quote the I have a dream speech without giving them the path to achieve their dreams

A dream becomes a goal when they can see themselves achieving it

Daniel Hale didn't wait for someone to approve the hospital he opened

Mark Dean didn't let black and white limit his vision to build a color monitor

Greatness doesn't wait for acceptance they create it

They planted themselves and make the ground fertile

They stand looking at their descendants

Hoping the leaves that fall will not rest on the ground unnoticed

This forest is too full of beautiful trees to be ignored

Don't do a drive by on history

Get out and look at the forgotten trees, their forgotten accomplishments, our forgotten history

It's not his-story it's our story

Know it

Live it

Respect it

FOUND

BUT LOST

I used to think a women should never be hit then I met you

Your black needs some blue to make it complete

My fist don't hit hard enough

I'm thirsty but your blood is the only thing I want to taste

I don't want another empty meaningless sorry

Lies, seeping from a tongue that knows the truth but seldom speaks it

You didn't want me or my sisters

So save your speeches

We've heard them all before

You want men

You only care about pleasing them

Why ae you so concerned with licking someone else's ass when yours is still dirty

Which uncle in in there this time

Uncles come then they go

You are wallowing in so much seamen that you can't see me

Us girls had to survive on our own

No comfort unless it was "Southern"

We drank to forget what we heard

We drank to forget you

We thought Marvin Gaye was a preacher

You see we heard let's get it on so much we thought it was a prayer

Your prayers answered but Uncle "fill in the blank"

No name needed, he wasn't going to be here that long

Did you ever stop for a moment and use your head instead of sucking on one

We aren't your children we are bracelets

Meant to adore your hand and removed as soon as you get home

Ignored until the next performance

Time to look impressive

Time to look like you care

Sunday church performance time

We know the routine and practice our lines

We're going to a new church so we have to perform especially well today

Isn't that uncle Monday night, he looks different

Must be the robe, priest collar and wife that look new

His wife rushes over to say hello

You sneak a sly smile at "uncle"

The wife's sister caught the glance

Now you are fighting lies and 2 sisters

No one comes to help a home wrecker

Not even us

Your plea softens my sister's giving heart and she comes to shield you

I run to shield my sister and soon there is a domino of sisters protecting each other

The fight ends by the sight of our innocence

We wanted you to get hit

To knock some sense into you

To break the lever that makes your legs open and your mind close

Praying maybe tonight will be our first night of solitude but when we get home Marvin sings and we drink

Disappointed that our reality did not change

We sisters plot another uncle reunion

Time to send another text message inviting you to your next beating

Hoping the next wife

Can fight better than the last one

YOU DON'T GET ME

I am so clear

I am so transparent

So why the dilemma

I don't think you get me

Why don't you see me

I told you everything you need to know

Why question me

I am secure in me

What are you questioning

I don't have a man

I don't need one to be happy

Really

You don't have one because you request too much

You push too much and you know too much

You spend your time examining him

You list his faults like they are lyrics to a song

But when it comes to yourself you can't sing a single note

How can you expect anyone to know you

When you don't even know yourself

Who are you

Don't expect me to find you

When you don't even realize that you are lost

You are not someone to wander past

You are someone to explore

You are worthy of your own time

Invest in you and stop running

He can't help you define you

Only you, God and a mirror can accomplish that

Stop asking a man to define you

Stop letting people label you

Your definition cannot run past someone else's lips

Only you can describe the inner workings that contain your soul

Dust off your thoughts

Look at yourself

Not your hair, size, or weight

Look at yourself

Don't rush

Take a moment

Know who you are

Know who you aren't

Work on who you want to be

But first you must say I am

And you must know what I am means

Let the excuses go

Take the "everyone else is" wrong suit off

Look solely at yourself

For in the end you define you

If someone else holds that power then once again you

have failed yourself

Decide who you are and revel in you,

I don't get you

Come back when you do

TRANS-
FORMERS

We are stepping and fetching for trappings not promises

Molded blackness projected at every turn

Don't want to be labeled:

The loud one, the proud one, the militant one, the fat ass one, the articulate one

Black ain't just one shade

But we've lowered ourselves

We moved to the valley

We have tainted our blackness with superficial vision

Let's look through this thin black veil and see another view

Men are more concerned with the depth or woman's ass instead of the depth of her knowledge

Women are looking for a rich baby daddy for themselves instead of a father for their children

Empire is a show we watch instead of something we build for ourselves

Lift every voice and sing is unknown but lift every skirt and twerk is seen daily

We say we are Christians but we quote Tupac, Biggie or Ray-Ray before we quote scripture

You don't miss an episode of Scandal but you can't make it to one parent teacher conference

You don't believe in wearing condoms but you don't believe in being a father either

You say you don't want people all up in your business but we're not the one posting your crap on Facebook you are

You have 4 DWI's but liquor ain't your problem, cops are

Your kids know all the words to "I'm in love with the Coco" but they don't what 2 time 9 equals

We have time to study blow job techniques but don't have enough time to study to get a GED

We got 99 problems and music is one

We sing I'm happy while fighting back tears

We are peacocks more worried about strutting then flying

We teach our sons to pick up a ball but not a pen

Our daughters are taught looking good is more important than being good

Our kids stand in line for $400 Jordans but can't point to Jordan on a map

Our black and white Bible sits unused but we know all 50 shades of gray

Our kids are encouraged to play doctors on TV but not be doctors in real life

If your child's first name has 10 syllables in it don't get hostile when someone abbreviates it (no one is trying to pronounce "Ladiaphragmeccialitcalisha" Smith)

We make sure we have a 50 inch TV but not a dime in a 401K

We tell our kids don't smoke and send them to the store to buy our cigarettes

We have $5000 rims on a $2000 car

We are walking bill boards for designers that don't care about us but we won't support an artist sitting 2 feet away

We overcame slavery to become slaves

America used to be optimus prime and we were transformers

We transformed this country and made it strong

Now we are nothing more than "transnegros"

Willingly changing to fit society

Bending into stereotypes

Unrecognizable in our true form

Trying to blend into America

Trying to be acceptable Negros

Death is the only time you can see a transnegro in their true form because death is black

Remember, you can't transform a corpse

Know that some of our misguided beliefs are from a learned view
Here is what we see
We've seen that the National Guard called out quickly to make sure we don't get out of line and slowly when we were stuck on flooded roofs
We've seen President Obama's birth certificate scrutinized more than Nixon's deceptions were publicized
It's okay if we play football in the NFL but we can't be the owner of a team
It's an academy award winning performance to play a thug but portraying Malcolm X is not worthy of a nomination
There are people who constantly hashtag all lives matter but when they took the ice bucket challenge they didn't hashtag all diseases matter
We are hunted, executed and killed for minor traffic offenses and some people are still saying well if you weren't speeding, walking or breathing you wouldn't get killed
We as a people have things to work on but making you comfortable with our skin is not one of them
I lifted this thin black veil to show you both sides
Now how do you like the view?

DEAR

DAD

I am not your excuse to make things right

I am not a living example for you to use

I am me

Why do you try so hard but do so little

I don't expect anything

I just want to exist on the same space you possess

You are so busy

Busy doing things that make you important

Important to others

You need not perform for me

I don't want it

I want you to see me

I want you to want to see me

No, I have no award

I'm not in a play

I just need your full vision for longer than a second

Look at me

Do not glance

Look at me

I want to matter to you

Don't rush pass me

Stop and sit

Make me matter

Make me yours

I am your child

Not a project that needs attention

Enjoy me now before I am gone

Growth and time will not hesitate to take me

Soon you will wonder

Where did the time go

It has not simply gone

You threw it away

I'M

BLACK

God formed me

I am African but you have ignored my race

Looked past my features

My rich deep brown soil holding life

My water runs deep

Brown trees cover me

Baring their nakedness with no shame

No matter how green the leaf is it is held in place by a brown branch

No matter how colorful the flower is it was cultivated in brown soil

When steel meets soil it eventually turns brown, its color overtaken

Breathe in God's artwork

See perfectly formed palates of pastels

Colors blended together to make earth bound rainbows visible

I bring you fruit

The darker the berry the more African the juice

I am Mother Nature and I am black

You may say black isn't part of the rainbow but there aren't too many colors you can make without black

Each time you see another color you see black but you look past it

If you found out that earth was black would you move or would black become acceptable

Some already know that the earth is black because...

You walk over her everyday but seldom bother to look down

You love the things she produces but don't give her any credit

You use her like she's your servant

You spit on her and call it water

You bury your garbage in her soil but you never acknowledge that you are the cause of her destruction

When will you recognize that you are killing her

You need her to survive

She keeps your buried secrets

Yet earth is slowly dying

Killing her softly still causes death but while she dies we fight

Why do we fight amongst ourselves

You don't see emeralds arguing with rubies

Yet they both sparkle

But we divide black into shades

Light in your skin starts questions of your "authenticity"

As if a bullet stops if your hue is light brown

Dark brown is "genuine" skin but deep black African skins' beauty is questioned

Yet no one steps outside at night and questions its beauty

We allow our beauty to be defined

We allow the world to tell us what's beautiful

We only look at ourselves as beautiful when they say so

Beauty is only skin deep but our culture is bone deep

We allow ourselves to be manipulated into dividing black into warring fractions

The earth is not immune

We have beaten this African planet so hard that she no longer produces like she used to

The whip that striped her soil hits all hue-mans

The disregard for her life kills us all

God named her earth and He also made her black

OUR

KIDS

Our seeds sprout

Walking even, talking like us

Looking at lessons we teach

Who have we taught them they need to be

Representatives of hate based on home grown prejudice

Non thinkers who follow a path even if a cliff appears

Grave diggers

Burying their secrets where no one can see

The only thing we showed them was that pain needs to hidden and screams need to be muffled to make everyone else comfortable

We show them how to shake hands but not how to take a stand

We have kids who can take a test but they cannot pass a life exam

What are we preparing them for

How to bend over

Our fruit is looking at a rotten tree

While trying to decide who they should be

What position are you in

They will duplicate what they see

Not just what you want them to be

Watch me do wrong but don't follow

Watch me shove pills down my throat but don't you swallow
You limit their oxygen by suffocating their dreams
The view from your pulpit has you forgetting your past
You walk around with dirty hands blaming your seed for considering the possibility that dirt is supposed to be on theirs
You want them to look in the mirror and love their reflection while you piss on any picture where their father is present
You were so happy they hated him that you overlooked the anger growing toward you
You can't teach hate and then limit its use
Hate does not stay in a lane
Once invited in it owns the highway
You can't be shocked at what they have done
Is the daughter a whore because of what she saw peering through her mother's bedroom door
You don't live in a bubble
Everything you do can later cause you trouble
You don't have a monopoly on pain but you're in denial
Denying that your kids pain is caused by you
Denying you're the initiator of hate

Overlooked truth doesn't change

You fertilized your seed with hate

Hate is now their way of life

Hate is your legacy

THE

BEATITUDES

Blessed are the truth tellers

For their words will help you grow

Blessed are those who are not willing to let you give up

For they will help you achieve great things

Blessed are those who make you see your potential

For they will insist that you expand your vision

Blessed are those who surround themselves with genuine friendship

For happiness is there's to the end of their days

Blessed are those who thirst for God

For they will drink from eternal waters

Blessed are those who are willing to admit their flaws

For they will overcome them

Blessed are those who explore their own pain

For their exploration will unearth the solution they need

Blessed are the parents

For they build foundations that can ensure strength

Blessed are the police officers and firefighters

For they run toward danger

Blessed are the teachers

For they mold young minds

Blessed are those who know they are blessed

For they will be a blessing to others

Blessed are those who have another day of life to enjoy

For they have time to repent and be saved

Blessed are those who listen

For they will be heard

Blessed are those who read

For knowledge will be their constant companion

If you want more, be a blessing to someone else

Expand their blessings

Explore the beauty that comes from giving to another

human being

Be a blessing

HAIKU

Pink Ribbon
Standing strong and firm,
pink ribbons transcend darkness
You are not alone

Be You
Try stopping the noise
Start with the lies you tell yourself
then you can be you

The Lord
First wait on the Lord
then listen to your soul speak
Your lessons are here

Lane
If someone tells you
get back in your lane, tell them
this is my highway

The Mind
You control your mind
or someone else will do it.
All thoughts start somewhere

Men
Men fight for what they
want, if you have to chase him
then he don't want you

Heart
Tranquilize your heart
so it will not affect you,
this is a slow death

Facts
Manipulation
is stretching facts to suit you.
Real truth needs nothing

Problem
Unsurmountable
destruction is not welcome
but we create it

KKK
Some of us would go
to a KKK rally
if the food was free

Exit
Some complications
got you ready to exit
Can't run from yourself

Love
Love me out of this
The pain is suffocating
Can't see, can't breathe, can't….

Battles
Beginning to see
battles are temporary
love is forever

Prayer
Walking with Jesus
it's a road worth traveling
bend down start today

Pain
Can't drown out problems
with liquor, needles or pills
Pain will wait for you

Love Gone
Love began to see
I was thirsty for the wrong
reasons so she left

Hate
Keeping hate alive
is throwing time to the wind
your time and your air

Strong Women
Strong women are not
unbreakable, we just know
you ain't the hammer

Drugs
If you're already
"tripping" off of drugs, you can't
fall for me, you're lost

Real
Milkshakes may bring boys
to the yard but real men are
going to want food

Rain
Don't make it rain at
a strip club, make it rain at
a homeless shelter

Choices
If you pick a guy
based on money, he can pick
you based on your ass

Burnt Churches
Burning down churches
you know the owner sees you
think, this is God's house

Love
Love can't conquer hate,
without conviction and faith
love is just a word

Empire
Why are you quoting
empire instead of building
one, focus on you

Truth
First lecture yourself
before you correct my ass
truth ain't just for me

God's Grace
Don't look upward when
pain grows but inward when joy
flows, God just saved you

Lust
Lust can't heal your heart
Looking for love on your back
Substitutes are fake

Partners
Slowing down your pace
to get her, why, if she can't
hustle leave her there

Limits
Remove your limits
You're blocking your own blessings
Expand your vision

KIMISM

Kimism

Don't waste time looking around to see who's watching

Haters will appear smaller in your rear view mirror

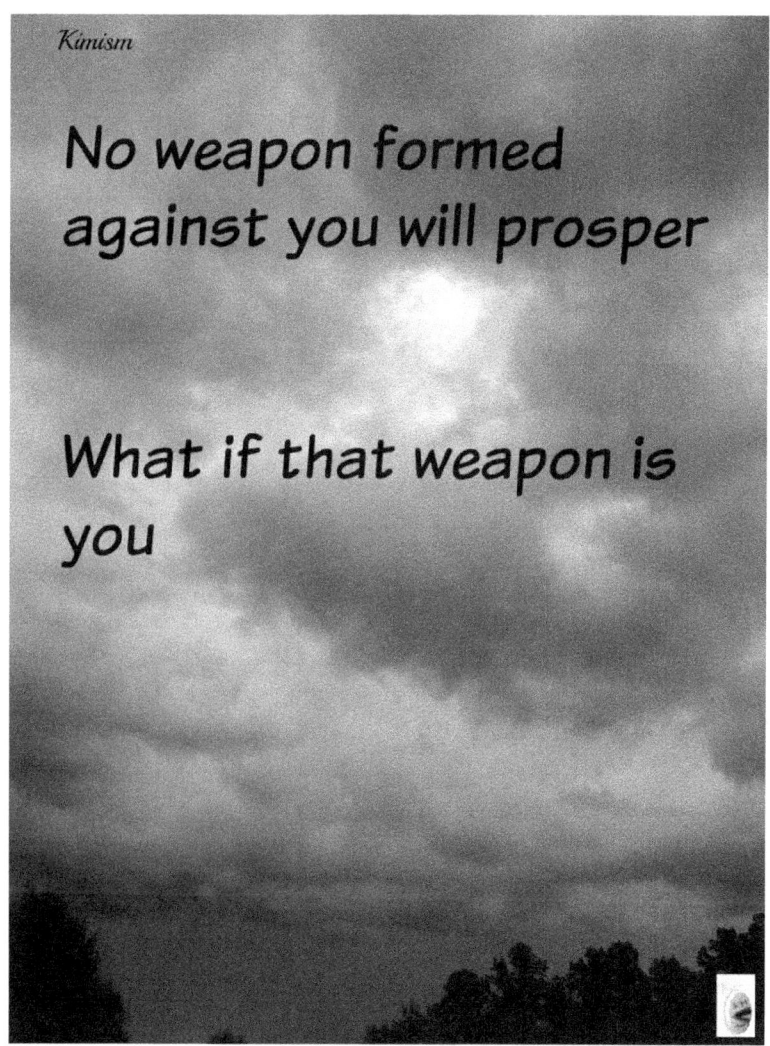

Kimism

No weapon formed against you will prosper

What if that weapon is you

Kimism

We call dogs & cats animals but they don't care if we're black, white, Asian, Latino, Native American...

Maybe we're the animals

Kimism

While you are trying to write inside the lines others are creating masterpieces

Make your own path

Kimism

If you don't know the whole story...

You don't know the story

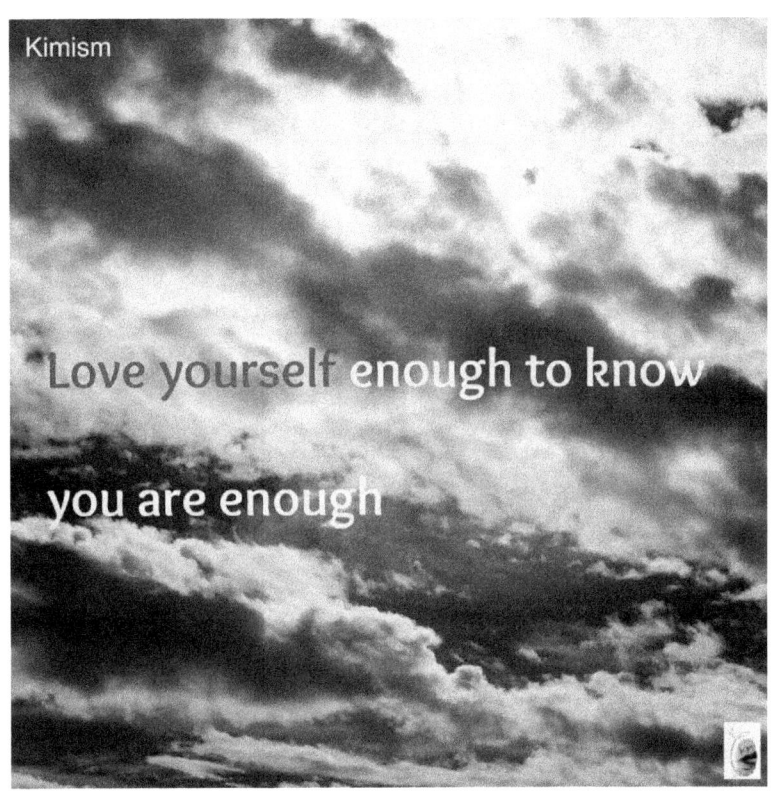

Kimism

When you were a kid you were fearless..

Now you fear more and live less

www.ingramcontent.com/pod-product-compliance
Lightning Source LLC
Chambersburg PA
CBHW050552300426
44112CB00013B/1886